W9-CMP-748

DISCARD

MATH MEASUREMENT WORD PROBLEMS: NO PROBLEM!

MATH BUSTERS
WORD PROBLEMS

Rebecca Wingard-Nelson

NEED
MORE PRACTICE?
free worksheets available at
http://www.enslow.com

E Enslow Publishers, Inc.

40 Industrial Road
Box 398
Berkeley Heights, NJ 07922
USA

http://www.enslow.com

Library of Congress Cataloging-in-Publication Data

Wingard-Nelson, Rebecca.
Math measurement word problems : no problem! / Rebecca Wingard-Nelson.
    p. cm. — (Math busters word problems)
Summary: "Presents a step-by-step guide to understanding word problems with math
measurement"— Provided by publisher.
 Includes bibliographical references and index.
 ISBN 978-0-7660-3369-6
1. Measurement—Juvenile literature. 2. Word problems (Mathematics)—Juvenile literature.   I.
Title.
QA465.W56 2011
516.0076—dc22
                        2010001119

Printed in the United States of America

052010 Lake Book Manufacturing, Inc., Melrose Park, IL

10 9 8 7 6 5 4 3 2 1

To Our Readers: We have done our best to make sure all Internet Addresses in this book were active and appropriate
when we went to press. However, the author and the publisher have no control over and assume no liability for the
material available on those Internet sites or on other Web sites they may link to. Any comments or suggestions can be
sent by e-mail to comments@enslow.com or to the address on the back cover.

♻ Enslow Publishers, Inc., is committed to printing our books on recycled paper. The paper in every book contains
10% to 30% post-consumer waste (PCW). The cover board on the outside of each book contains 100% PCW. Our goal
is to do our part to help young people and the environment too!

Illustration credits: © Comstock/PunchStock, p. 7; © Corbis Corporation, pp. 9, 49; Shutterstock, pp. 5, 11, 13, 14,
17, 19, 21, 22, 25, 26, 28, 30, 31, 33, 35, 37, 38, 41, 43, 45, 47, 51, 53, 54, 57, 58, 61; U.S. Department of Interior,
p. 56.

Cover Photo: Shutterstock

Free Worksheets are available for this book at http://www.enslow.com. Search on the *Math Busters Word Problems*
series name. The publisher will provide access to the worksheets for five years from the book's first publication date.

Contents

Introduction   5

1. Problem-Solving Tips   6

2. Problem-Solving Steps   8

3. Measurement Basics   10

4. Length: Standard Units   12

5. Converting to Larger Units   14

6. Use a Fraction   16

7. Length: Metric Units   18

8. Estimating Length   20

9. Adding and Subtracting Measurements   22

10. Perimeter   24

11. Area   26

12. Capacity   28

13. Metric Capacity   30

14. Error in Measurement   32

15. Volume   34

16. Change Dimensions 36

17. Weight or Mass 38

18. Weight 40

19. Use Mental Math 42

20. Estimating Weight 44

21. Read a Graph 46

22. Use a Table 48

23. Time Basics 50

24. Calendars 52

25. Elapsed Time 54

26. Time Zones 56

27. Mixed Measures 58

28. More Mixed Measures 60

Further Reading 62

Internet Addresses 62

Index 63

Introduction

How much longer until dinner? How far is it around the park? How fast will that car go? Time, distance, and speed are some types of measurements that are used in math. Math is everywhere; you just might not realize it all the time because math isn't always written as a math problem.

This book will help you understand how measurement is used in word problems. The step-by-step method can help students, parents, teachers, and tutors solve any word problem. It can be read from beginning to end or used to review a specific topic. Let's get started!

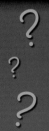# ① Problem-Solving Tips

How do I start? What do I do if I get stuck?
What if the answer is wrong when I check it?
Word problems are hard for me!

Get Involved!

You can watch a swim meet and see swimmers racing across a pool. But if you want to learn how to swim, you must get in the water. Solving math problems is not a spectator sport. You may first watch how others solve word problems, but then you need to solve them for yourself, too. Go ahead, jump in!

Practice!

Even the most gifted athlete or musician will tell you that in order to play well, you must practice. The more you practice anything, the better and faster you become at it. The same is true for problem solving. Homework problems and class work are your practice.

Learning Means <u>Not</u> Already Knowing!

If you already know everything, there is nothing left to learn. Every mistake you make is a potential learning experience. When you understand a problem and get the right answer the first time, good for you! When you do NOT understand a problem but figure it out, or you make a mistake and learn from it, AWESOME for you!

Questions, Questions!

Ask smart questions. Whoever is helping you does not know what you don't understand unless you tell them. You must ask a question before you can get an answer.

Ask questions early. Concepts in math build on each other. Today's material is essential for understanding tomorrow's.

Don't Give Up!

Stuck on homework? There are many resources for homework help.
* Check a textbook.
* Ask someone who does understand.
* Try looking up sources on the Internet (but don't get distracted).
* Read this book!

Getting frustrated? Take a break.
* Get a snack or a drink of water.
* Move around and get your blood flowing. Then come back and try again.

Stuck on a test? If you do get stuck on a problem, move on to the next one. Solve the problems you understand first. That way, you won't miss the problems you do understand because you were stuck on one you didn't. If you have time, go back and try the ones you skipped.

Wrong answer? Check the math; it could be a simple mistake. Try solving the problem another way. There are many problem-solving strategies, and usually more than one of them will work. Don't give up. If you quit, you won't learn anything.

② Problem-Solving Steps

What steps can I take to solve word problems? If I follow the steps, will I be more likely to get a correct answer? Will I have less trouble finding the answer?

Problem-Solving Steps

Step 1: Understand the problem.
Step 2: Make a plan.
Step 3: Follow the plan.
Step 4: Review.

Step 1: Understand the problem.

Read the problem. Read the problem again. This may seem obvious, but this step may be the most important.

Ask yourself questions like:
Do I understand all of the words in the problem?
Can I restate the problem in my own words?
Will a picture or diagram help me understand the problem?
What does the problem ask me to find or show?
What information do I need to solve the problem?
Do I have all of the information I need?

Underlining the important information can help you to understand the problem. Read the problem as many times as it takes for you to have a clear sense of what happens in the problem and of what you are asked to find.

Step 2: Make a plan.

There are many ways to solve a math problem. Choosing a good plan becomes easier as you solve more problems. Some plans you may choose are:

Make a list. *Guess and check.*
Draw a picture. *Work backward.*
Use logical reasoning. *Solve a simpler problem.*
Use what you know. *Use a number line or graph.*
Use a model. *Use a table.*

When there is a computation, such as addition or subtraction, an important plan is **write an equation**. When this is the plan, the main task at this step is to choose the correct operation.

Step 3: Follow the plan.

Now that you understand the problem and have decided how to solve it, you can carry out your plan. Use the plan you have chosen. If it does not work, go back to step 2 and choose a different plan.

Step 4: Review.

Look over the problem and your answer. Does the answer match the question? Does the answer make sense? Is it reasonable? Check the math. What plan worked or did not work? Looking back at what you have done on this problem will help you solve similar problems.

③ Measurement Basics

Two systems of measurement, standard and metric, are used for most measures. These systems are used for measures of length, capacity, weight or mass, area, and volume.

Standard Measures

The standard system of measurement, or customary system, is based on early English measurement units. Some of the most common standard measurement units are listed below. The abbreviation for each is shown in parentheses.

Length

12 inches (in) = 1 foot (ft)

3 feet = 1 yard (yd)

5,280 feet = 1 mile (mi)

Capacity

8 ounces = 1 cup (c)

2 cups = 1 pint (pt)

2 pints = 1 quart (qt)

4 quarts = 1 gallon (gal)

Mass/Weight

16 ounces (oz) = 1 pound (lb)

To help you understand the size of some standard units, here are some examples:

The diameter of a quarter is about an inch.
A yard is about the length of an adult's arm.
A slice of bread weighs about one ounce.
A loaf of bread weighs about one pound.

In some cultures, a similar word to inch means thumb. In others cultures, a similar word to inch means twelfth (as in one twelfth of a foot).

Metric Measures

The metric system uses multiples of ten and a base unit for each type of measurement. For example, the base unit to measure length is a meter. A prefix is added to the word *meter* to show a different unit of length. A meter is 10 times as long as a **deci**meter. A **kilo**meter is 1,000 times as long as a meter.

Base units, common prefixes, and the value for each prefix are listed below. The abbreviation for each is shown in parentheses. Metric unit abbreviations include the prefix and the base unit. For example, millimeters are abbreviated as mm.

Base Units

Length:	Capacity:	Mass:
meter (m)	liter (l)	gram (g)

Prefix	Value
nano- (n)	one billionth of a base unit
micro- (mc or u)	one millionth of a base unit
milli- (m)	one thousandth of a base unit
centi- (c)	one hundredth of a base unit
deci- (d)	one tenth of a base unit
deca- (da)	ten base units
kilo- (k)	one thousand base units
mega- (M)	one million base units
giga- (G)	one billion base units

To help you understand the size of some metric units, here are some examples:

The thickness of a dime is about a millimeter.
The width of a fingernail is about a centimeter.
A meter is a little longer than a yard, but both
   are about the length of an adult's arm.
A paper clip has the mass of about a gram.
A milliliter is about 10 drops.

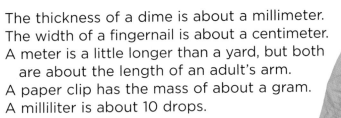

Cheryl is 5 feet tall. How tall is Cheryl in inches?

Step 1: Understand the problem.

Read the problem. Restate the question in your own words.
What is Cheryl's height in inches?

What does the problem ask you to find?
The number of inches in 5 feet.

What information do you need to solve the problem?
Cheryl's height and the number of inches in a foot.

Do you have all of the information that you need?
The problem does not tell you the number of inches in a foot. Measurement problems often expect you to know how different units are related. There are 12 inches in a foot.

Step 2: Make a plan.

Let's start with a drawing to understand the problem.

Step 3: Follow the plan.

Let's use a line that is separated into five sections, one for each foot of height, to show Cheryl's height.

Each foot is the same as 12 inches. By looking at the drawing, you can tell that if you add 12 inches for each foot, you can find Cheryl's total height in inches.

12 + 12 + 12 + 12 + 12 = 60

Cheryl is 60 inches tall.

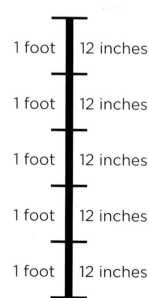

1 foot   12 inches

1 foot   12 inches

1 foot   12 inches

1 foot   12 inches

1 foot   12 inches

Step 4: Review.

Does the answer match the question?
Yes, the problem asked for a height in inches.

Does the answer make sense?
Yes, there are more inches than feet.

Is there another way you can solve this problem?
Yes. Problems that ask you to convert from a larger unit (feet) to a smaller unit (inches) can be solved using whole number multiplication. Multiply the number of large units by the number of smaller units that are in each larger unit.

number of feet times
number of inches per foot equals
number of inches

5 × 12 = 60

There are more small units in a given amount than large units.

When you change from feet to inches, the value for inches should be larger than the one for feet.

Malik ran the football 150 feet for a touchdown. In yards, how far did Malik run the football?

Step 1: Understand the problem.

Read the problem. Is there anything you do not understand?

What does the problem ask you to find?
The number of yards that Malik ran with the football to score a touchdown.

What information do you need to solve the problem?
The number of feet Malik ran and the number of feet in a yard.

Do you have all of the information that you need?
The problem does not tell you the number of feet in a yard. You must know that 3 feet is equal to 1 yard.

Step 2: Make a plan.

You are changing feet to yards. To change from a smaller unit to a larger unit, you can use whole number division. Let's write a division equation to solve this problem.

Step 3: Follow the plan.

One way to write an equation is to write words first, then change the words to numbers and math symbols.

number of feet divided by feet per yard equals number of yards

150 ÷ 3 = 50

Malik ran the football 50 yards.

Step 4: Review.

Does the answer match the question?
Yes, the problem asked for a number of yards.

Did the plan work for the problem? **Yes.**

Because yards are larger than feet, you can expect that you will have fewer yards than you had feet. Malik ran 150 feet. Is your answer fewer than 150 yards? **Yes, 50 is fewer than 150.**

To convert from larger to smaller units, multiply by a whole number. The answer will be greater than the original value.

To convert from smaller to larger units, divide by a whole number. The answer will be less than the original value.

⑥ Use a Fraction

Jess bought 1,760 feet of ribbon for the color guard. How many miles of ribbon did she buy?

Step 1: Understand the problem.

Read the problem. Is there anything you do not understand?

What does the problem ask you to find?
The amount of ribbon in miles that Jess bought.

What information do you need to solve the problem? Is all of the information that you need in the question?
You need to know how many feet of ribbon Jess has and the number of feet in a mile. The problem does not tell you the number of feet in a mile. There are 5,280 feet in a mile.

Step 2: Make a plan.

Another way to convert from smaller to larger units to is to use a fraction. Let's use a fraction.

Step 3: Follow the plan.

Fractions show what part you have out of a whole thing. The part can be any amount, but the whole is always the number of parts in one whole thing. Look at this example.

You want to convert 2 feet to a number of yards. You know there are 3 feet in one yard.

$\dfrac{\text{part}}{\text{whole}}$	$\dfrac{\text{number of feet you have}}{\text{number of feet in one yard}}$	$\dfrac{2}{3}$

So, 2 feet is 2/3 of a yard.

Use this example to write a fraction for your word problem.

16

part	number of feet you have	1,760
whole	number of feet in a whole mile	5,280

Reduce the fraction to lowest terms.

$$\frac{1,760}{5,280} = \frac{1}{3}$$

Jess bought 1/3 mile of ribbon.

Step 4: Review.

Does the answer match the question? **Yes. The problem asked for a number of miles.**

Does the answer make sense? **Yes. There are 5,280 feet in one mile. Jess bought less than 5,280 feet, so she bought less than one mile of ribbon.**

Did the plan work for the problem? **Yes.**

A 5K race is called a 5K because the race is 5 kilometers long. How many meters long is a 5K race?

Step 1: Understand the problem.

Read the problem. Is there anything you do not understand?

What does the problem ask you to find?
The number of meters in 5-kilometer race.

What information do you need to solve the problem?
You need to know the number of meters in a kilometer. The chart on page 11 tells you there are 1,000 meters in a kilometer.

Multiplying and Dividing by Powers of Ten

Powers of ten are numbers that are found by multiplying ten by itself a given number of times.
100 is 10 to the 2nd power because it is 10 x 10.
1,000 is 10 to the 3rd power because 1,000 = 10 x 10 x 10.

To multiply a number by a power of ten, move the decimal point right the same number of places as there are zeros.
$0.04 \times 10 = 0.4$ $0.04 \times 100 = 4$ $0.04 \times 1,000 = 40$

To divide a number by a power of ten, move the decimal point left the same number of places as there are zeros.
$2.0 \div 10 = 0.2$ $2.0 \div 100 = 0.02$ $2.0 \div 1,000 = 0.002$

Step 2: Make a plan.

Metric lengths can be converted using mental math. You can simply move the decimal point in the original value.

Step 3: Follow the plan.

The chart on page 11 tells you there are 1,000 meters in one kilometer. Multiply to convert from larger units to smaller units. To multiply by a power of 10, you can move the decimal point right the same number of places as there are zeros. There are three zeros in 1,000, so move the decimal point right three places. In a whole number, the decimal point is at the right end.

Think: 1,000 × 5 = 5000

A 5K race is 5,000 meters long.

Step 4: Review.

Does the answer match the question?
Yes. The problem asked the number of meters.

If you were given the number of meters in a race, how could you convert to kilometers? **Use division. When you divide by a power of ten the decimal point moves left. There are 1,000 meters in one kilometer. If the race is 3,000 meters long, move the decimal point left three places.**

3,000 meters = 3.000 kilometers

⑧ Estimating Length

Step 1: Understand the problem.

Read the problem. Is there anything you do not understand?

What does the problem ask you to find?
A measurement for the height of this book.

What information do you need to solve the problem?
The book, and a way to find its height.

Step 2: Make a plan.

Estimation problems ask you to find an answer that is close to the exact answer. Problems that use words such as *approximately, around, estimate, guess, nearly,* and *roughly* may tell you the problem is an estimation problem. This problem uses the word *about*. Estimate the height of the book.

Step 3: Follow the plan.

To estimate the height of this book, first decide what units you want to use. Let's use customary units. The book height is less than the length of your arm, so it is less than a yard. It is probably less than a third of your arm, so it is less than a foot. It is greater than the width of a quarter, so it is more than one inch. Inches are the best unit to use to estimate the height.

Now choose how to estimate the measurement. Let's use quarters. The diameter of a quarter is just a little less than an inch.

How many quarters will fit side by side along the edge of the book? **About nine.**

This book is about 9 inches tall.

Step 4: Review.

Does the answer match the question? **Yes. The problem asked for an estimate of the height of this book.**

Did the plan work for the problem? **Yes.**

Check your estimate using a ruler. **The book is a little over 9 inches tall. It is a good estimate.**

Is there another plan you can use to solve the problem? **Yes. You could have chosen to use your thumb or another item with a measurement close to an inch to estimate the height. Or you could have used feet as the unit and found the estimate in fractions of a foot. You also may have chosen to estimate the height in metric units.**

⑨ Adding and Subtracting Measurements

Jin wants the tallest Christmas tree he can put in his living room. The ceiling is 9 meters high. He needs a total of 18 centimeters for the tree stand and tree topper. How tall can the tree be?

Step 1: Understand the problem.

Read the problem. Is there anything you do not understand? What does the problem ask you to find?
The greatest height that a Christmas tree can be and still fit in Jin's living room.

What do you need to solve the problem?
The ceiling height and how much room is needed above and below the tree.

Step 2: Make a plan.

This problem tells you the height of the room and the amount of that height that cannot be used for the height. This is a subtraction problem. Write a subtraction equation.

This problem uses indirect measurement. Direct measurement compares an object directly to a measuring device (like a ruler or a scale). Indirect measurement finds a measurement by using the measurements of something else.

Step 3: Follow the plan.

The problem asks the height of the tallest tree that will fit in Jin's living room. To find that height, you can begin with the height of the living room and subtract the amount of room that is needed for the tree stand and tree topper.

height of room minus room needed equals height left for tree

9 m − 18 cm = height left for tree

Measurements being added or subtracted MUST have the same units. Convert meters to centimeters by multiplying by 100.

900 cm − 18 cm = height left for tree

900 cm − 18 cm = 882 cm

The tallest tree Jin can buy can be 882 cm tall.

Step 4: Review.

Does the answer match the question?
Yes. The problem asked for a height.

Did the plan work for the problem? **Yes.**

Can the answer be given in another way? **Yes. You could convert to other metric units, such as meters instead of centimeters.**

9 m - 0.18 m = 8.82 m

8.82 m = 882 cm

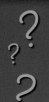

⑩ Perimeter

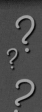

Every morning, Quinton walks his dog along the perimeter of his rectangular yard. The yard is 216 feet wide and 160 feet long. What is the perimeter of the yard?

Step 1: Understand the problem.

Read the problem. Is there anything you do not understand? What is a perimeter? **A perimeter is the length of all the sides of a shape.**

What does the problem ask you to find?
The perimeter of Quinton's yard.

What information do you need to solve the problem?
The length of each side of the yard.

Step 2: Make a plan.

The perimeter of a shape is found by adding the length of each side. Write an equation that adds the length of each side.

Step 3: Follow the plan.

The problem tells you the yard is a rectangle. A rectangle has four sides, with two sets of sides that have the same length. It may help to draw a sketch of the yard with the length of each side noted.

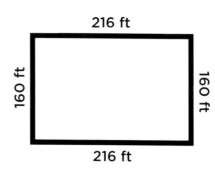

24

Use the drawing to help write the equation.

side 1 plus side 2 plus side 3 plus side 4 equals perimeter

216 ft + 160 ft + 216 ft + 160 ft = perimeter

Do the addition. All of the lengths use the same unit, feet, so there is no need to convert units.

216 ft + 160 ft + 216 ft + 160 ft = 752 ft

The perimeter of Quinton's yard is 752 feet.

Step 4: Review.

Does the answer match the question?
Yes. The problem asked for a distance, or length.

Did you remember to include the units in your answer? **Yes.**

Is there another way to solve the problem? **Yes. You could have used multiplication to double the length of each of the equal sides, then added the products.**

216 × 2 = 432   160 × 2 = 320   432 + 320 = 752 ft

⑪ Area

Chase and Freddie each claim the poster they made to advertise their band's show is bigger. Chase's poster is 8 inches wide and 18 inches tall. Freddie's poster is 16 inches wide and 9 inches tall. Which poster is bigger?

Step 1: Understand the problem.

Read the problem. Chase made a taller poster, but Freddie made a wider poster. How can you compare the size of the two posters? **This problem is not asking which poster is taller or wider. The word bigger in this problem is asking which poster covers more space. The size of the surface that is covered is called area.**

What does the problem ask you to find?
Which poster is bigger, or has the most area.

Do you have all of the information you need to solve the problem?
Yes, you know the height and width of each poster.

Step 2: Make a plan.

This is a comparison problem.
Find the area of each poster.
Then compare the areas.

When you multiply or divide two measurement units that are the same type (two lengths, two weights, two times), be sure the units are the same. For example, only multiply inches by inches, or feet by feet. Do NOT multiply feet by inches.

Step 3: Follow the plan.

Area is measured in square units.
For example, a square inch
(sq in or in^2) is a square that
is one inch tall and one inch wide.
The area of a rectangle can be found by
multiplying the length (height) by the width.
Find the area of each poster.

Chase's poster area = 18 in × 8 in = 144 in^2

Freddie's poster area = 9 in × 16 in = 144 in^2

In this problem, each poster has the same area.

Neither poster is bigger, they have the same area.

Step 4: Review.

Does the answer match the question?
Yes. The problem did not ask for a number. It asked which poster was bigger.

Why can you multiply the
length and width to find
the area?
**Look at the simple example
of a 4-inch-wide by 3-inch-
high area. You can count
12 square inches. Or you
can picture the rectangle
as 3 rows of 4 square inches.
Three sets of four can be
found using multiplication.
3 × 4 = 12**

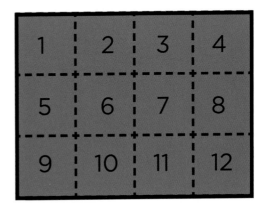

⑫ Capacity

Once a week Cici waters the saplings that she is donating to a city park. Each sapling gets 3 pints of water. If Cici has 32 saplings, how much water does she use each week?

Step 1: Understand the problem.

Read the problem. Is there anything you do not understand?
What is a sapling? **A sapling is a young tree. You do NOT need to know what a sapling is to solve the problem.**

What does the problem ask you to find?
The amount of water Cici uses in a week to water the saplings.

What information do you need to solve the problem?
The number of saplings and the amount of water each receives.

Step 2: Make a plan.

You are given the amount of water one sapling gets, and asked to find the amount of water 32 saplings get. This is a multiplication problem. Write a multiplication equation.

Step 3: Follow the plan.

Write the equation in words first.

<u>number of saplings</u> <u>times</u> <u>water per sapling</u> <u>equals</u> <u>total water</u>

Replace the words with numbers. Then multiply.

32 × 3 = total water

Since 32 has more than one digit use columns to multiply.

$$\begin{array}{r} 32 \\ \times\ 3 \\ \hline 96 \end{array}$$

Cici uses 96 pints of water each week.

Although the answer is acceptable in pints, the number of pints is very large. A better answer could be given by converting the pints to gallons.

There are 8 pints in one gallon. Divide the answer by 8 to find the number of gallons.

96 pints ÷ 8 pints per gallon = 12 gallons
Cici uses 12 gallons of water each week.

Step 4: Review.

Does the answer match the question?
Yes. The problem asked for an amount of water.

Why is the answer given in units of capacity and not weight?
Liquids, such as water, milk, and motor oil, are usually measured using capacity, or how much of something a given container can hold. Liquids can also be measured using weight, but the problem gives you a unit of capacity, so the answer should also be in units of capacity.

Elaine poured 4 liters of pop from 2-liter bottles into a set of 50 glasses. Each glass has a capacity of 2 deciliters. How many glasses did she fill before she ran out of pop?

Step 1: Understand the problem.

Read the problem. Is there anything you do not understand?

What does the problem ask you to find?
The number of glasses Elaine filled.

Do you have all of the information you need to solve the problem?
Yes. You know the total amount Elaine poured and the amount that went into each glass.

Is there extra information?
Yes. You do not need to know that the pop was in 2-liter bottles. You also do not need to know that she has a set of 50 glasses.

Step 2: Make a plan.

This problem tells you that 4 liters of pop were divided into glasses that hold 2 deciliters each.
Problems that start with a large value and divide it into equal smaller values are often division problems.

Let's write a division equation.

Step 3: Follow the plan.

Write the equation in words first.

total pop **divided by** **amount per glass** **equals** **number of glasses**

4 liters ÷ 2 deciliters = number of glasses filled

Before you divide, the measurements must have the same units.
Convert liters to deciliters by multiplying by 10.

40 dl ÷ 2 dl = number of glasses filled

40 dl ÷ 2 dl = 20 glasses filled

Elaine filled 20 glasses before she ran out of pop.

Step 4: Review.

Does your answer match the question?
Yes. The problem asked for the number of glasses Elaine filled.

Check your answer.
You can use multiplication to check the answer to division problems. Multiply your answer by the number you divided by.

20 × 2 = 40
There are 40 dl in 4 liters, the amount you started with.

⑭ Error in Measurement

Sarah is using a graduated cylinder that is marked in milliliters. How far off can Sarah's measurement be from exact without being incorrect when she measures to the nearest milliliter?

Step 1: Understand the problem.

Read the problem. What does the problem ask you to find?
The amount of error in measurement Sarah can have without being incorrect.

What information do you need to solve the problem?
The smallest unit that is marked on the beaker, or the precision of the beaker.

Error in Measurement

Measurements made with a measuring device are never exact. You can measure the same item two different times, and the result may not be exactly the same.

The **precision** of a measuring instrument is the smallest fractional or decimal division marked on the scale of the instrument. If the smallest units on a ruler are millimeters, the precision is given as "to the nearest millimeter."

The **greatest possible error** in a measurement should be half of the measuring device's precision. If the precision is to the nearest inch, the greatest possible error should be half an inch.

Step 2: Make a plan.

Let's look at a beaker and use logical reasoning.

Step 3: Follow the plan.

This graduated cylinder is marked in milliliters. To the nearest milliliter, there are 46 ml of liquid. What is the greatest amount of liquid that could still be read as 46 ml?
Just less than 46.5 ml, or 46 1/2 ml.

Why?
If there are 46.5 ml or more, the measurement is read as 47 ml.

What is the least amount of liquid that could still be read as 46 ml?
45.5 ml, or 45 1/2 ml.

Why?
If there are less than 45.5 ml, the measurement is read as 45 ml.

What is the greatest difference between the exact measure and the measurement that is read as "to the nearest milliliter"?
0.5 ml, or 1/2 ml.

Sarah's measurement can be up to half a milliliter from exact and be correct.

Step 4: Review.

Does the answer match the question?
Yes. The problem asked for the greatest possible error.

⑮ Volume

The cargo area on Cindi's pickup truck measures 3 meters long by 2 meters wide by 1 meter deep. When the cargo area is enclosed, how many cubic meters of cargo will fit in the enclosed space?

Step 1: Understand the problem.

Read the problem. Is there anything you do not understand? What is a cubic meter? **A cubic meter is a measuring unit for volume. It is the space taken up by a cube with a side length of one meter.**

What does the problem ask you to find? **The volume of the cargo area when the area is enclosed.**

What information do you need to solve the problem? **The length, width, and height of the cargo area.**

Capacity is the amount that can fit into something. The capacity of a box could be 2 cups.

Volume is the amount of space something takes up. The volume of a box could be 8 cubic inches.

Formulas

A **formula** is a mathematical rule that is written using symbols or general words. The formula to find the area of a rectangle is Area = length × width, or $A = lw$. To solve a problem using a formula, substitute values from the problem into the formula.

34

Step 2: Make a plan.

The cargo area of the truck is a rectangular prism. You can use a formula to find the volume of the cargo area.

Step 3: Follow the plan.

The formula for the volume of a rectangular prism is

Volume = length × width × height

Replace the words with numbers from the problem. Then multiply.

Volume = 3 m × 2 m × 1 m = 6 m^3

The enclosed cargo area of the truck will hold 6 cubic meters of cargo.

Step 4: Review.

Check your answer. **You can draw a picture to check your answer. Draw a set of cubes in a rectangle that is 3 cubes long and 2 cubes wide. Since the cargo area is 1 meter high, only draw one layer. Count the cubes. There are 6.**

⑯ Change Dimensions

Gerard built a robot that carries a 2-cm cube. Cynthia built a robot that carries a 4-cm cube. How many times larger is the volume of the 4-cm cube than the 2-cm cube?

Step 1: Understand the problem.

Read the problem. What does the problem ask you to find?
The number of times larger the 4-cm cube is than the 2-cm cube.

What information do you need to solve the problem?
The size of each cube.

Is all of the information that you need in the question? **Yes.**

A 2-cm cube is a cube that is 2 centimeters on each edge.

Step 2: Make a plan.

This problem asks you to compare the volumes of two cubes. You can break the problem into more than one part.
First find the volume of each cube. Then compare the volumes.

Step 3: Follow the plan.

Find the volume of each cube. The volume of a cube is found by multiplying the side length three times.

Volume of 2-cm cube = 2 cm × 2 cm × 2 cm = 8 cm^3
Volume of 4-cm cube = 4 cm × 4 cm × 4 cm = 64 cm^3

The problem asks for the number of times larger the volume of the larger cube is than the smaller one. Use division to compare the volumes.

64 cm^3 ÷ 8 cm^3 = 8

The volume of the 4-cm cube is 8 times larger than the volume of the 2-cm cube.

Step 4: Review.

Does the answer match the question?
Yes. The problem asked for comparison.

The side length of the cube is doubled (2 times larger), but the volume is 8 times larger. Why is this the case?
Length is one-dimensional. If you double a length, it becomes two times as long.

Area is two-dimensional. If you double the length of each side, the area becomes 4 times as large (2 × 2).

Volume is three-dimensional. If you double the length of each side, the volume becomes 8 times as large (2 × 2 × 2).

⑰ Weight or Mass

Josie's weight on Earth is 120 pounds. The force of gravity on Mars is only about 1/3 of the force of gravity on Earth. If Josie went to Mars and stood on a scale, how much would she weigh?

Step 1: Understand the problem.

Read the problem. Is there anything you do not understand?
Why does your weight change?
Weight is a measure that includes the force of gravity. When the force of gravity changes, the weight of an object changes by the same factor.

What does the problem ask you to find?
The amount Josie would weigh on Mars.

What information do you need to solve the problem? **Josie's weight and the difference in gravity between Mars and Earth.**

Step 2: Make a plan.

The problem tells you the force of gravity on Mars is about 1/3 the force of gravity on Earth. This means Josie's weight on Mars will be about 1/3 of her weight on Earth. The word *of* indicates you can find her weight on Mars using multiplication.
Write a multiplication equation.

Mass, Weight, and Gravity

Mass is a measurement of the amount of matter an object contains. Matter is different from volume. Two objects with the same volume can have a different mass because one contains more matter. Think of it like packing two of the same sized suitcases. You can fill one with clothes that are loosely packed and stuff the other full. One contains more matter, so it has greater mass, but the volumes are the same.

Weight is a measurement that depends on the pull of gravity. Gravity does not change the mass of an object, because the amount of matter in the object does not change.

Step 3: Follow the plan.

Write the problem in words.

fraction of weight on Earth **equals** **weight on Mars**

Replace the words with numbers and symbols.

$1/3 \times 120$ pounds = weight on Mars

Multiply.

$1/3 \times 120$ pounds = 40 pounds
Josie would weigh about 40 pounds on Mars.

Step 4: Review.

Does the answer match the question? **Yes. The problem asked how much Josie would weigh if she stepped on a scale on Mars.**

Is your answer exact? **No. Although you did not estimate to find the answer, the problem tells you that the weight on Mars is** *about* **1/3 the weight on Earth. The factor is not exactly 1/3, so the answer is not exact.**

Does the answer make sense? **Yes. Josie's weight on Mars is about 1/3 of her weight. That means she weighs three times as much on Earth as she would on Mars. Her weight, 120 pounds, is three times 40 pounds.**

⑱ Weight

Marc's laptop weighs 4.75 pounds. What is the weight of Marc's laptop in ounces?

Step 1: Understand the problem.

Read the problem. What does the problem ask you to find?
The weight of Marc's laptop in ounces.

What information do you need to solve the problem?
The weight of the laptop in pounds and the number of ounces in one pound.

Step 2: Make a plan.

Pounds are larger (heavier) units than ounces.
Any measurements can be converted from larger units to smaller units using multiplication.

Step 3: Follow the plan.

Multiply the number of larger units by the number of smaller units in one larger unit. Write the problem in words.

<u>number of pounds</u> <u>times</u> <u>number of ounces per pound</u> <u>equals</u> <u>number of ounces</u>

There are 16 ounces in a pound. Memorize some of the basic unit conversions, such as the number of inches in a foot, ounces in a pound, and quarts in a gallon. Other measurement conversion factors can be found in tables, books, or by looking them up on the Internet.

Replace the words with numbers and symbols.

4.75 $\times$ 16 = number of ounces

40

$$
\begin{array}{r}
4\ 3 \\
\mathbf{4.75} \\
\times\ \ \ \mathbf{16} \\
\hline
\mathbf{2850} \\
+\ \mathbf{4750} \\
\hline
\mathbf{76.00}
\end{array}
$$

Marc's laptop weighs 76 ounces.

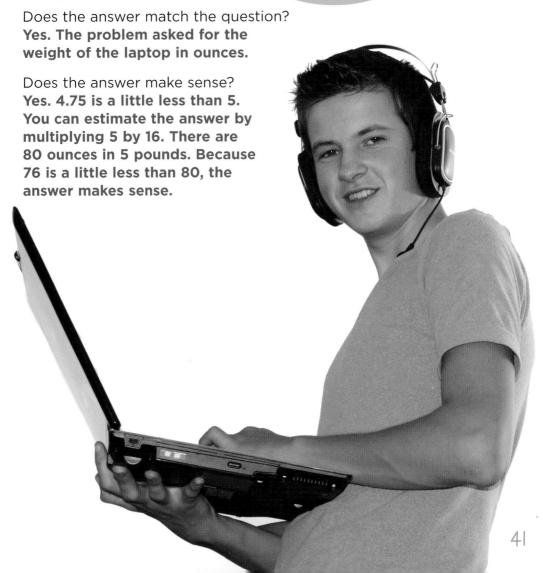

To multipy decimals, ignore the decimal point.

Count the places on the right of the decimal point in the factors.

Put a decimal point in the answer so that there are the same number of places on the right.

Step 4: Review.

Does the answer match the question? **Yes. The problem asked for the weight of the laptop in ounces.**

Does the answer make sense? **Yes. 4.75 is a little less than 5. You can estimate the answer by multiplying 5 by 16. There are 80 ounces in 5 pounds. Because 76 is a little less than 80, the answer makes sense.**

41

⑲ Use Mental Math

The mass of a penny is 2.5 grams. The mass of a nickel is 5 grams. How many pennies are in a bag containing 1 kilogram of pennies?

Step 1: Understand the problem.

Read the problem. What does the problem ask you to find?
The number of pennies in the bag.

What information do you need to solve the problem?
The mass of one penny and the mass of the pennies in the bag.

Step 2: Make a plan.

You know the total mass contained in the bag of pennies. You know the mass of one penny. You can find the number of pennies using mental math and division.

Step 3: Follow the plan.

The mass of the pennies in the bag is given in kilograms. The mass of one penny is given in grams.

Think: There are 1,000 grams in 1 kilogram.

Think: It is easier to find the number of nickels that make up 1,000 grams. Mentally divide: 1,000 ÷ 5 = 200. It takes 200 nickels to equal the mass of 1 kilogram.

Think: The mass of two pennies is the same as the mass of one nickel. Double the number of nickels to find the number of pennies.
It takes 200 nickels to equal the mass of 400 pennies.

There are about 400 pennies in the bag.

Step 4: Review.

Does the answer match the question?
Yes. The problem asked for the number of pennies in the bag.

Check the math.
Multiply the number of pennies in the answer, 400, by the number of grams in one penny, 2.5.

$400 \times 2.5 = 1,000$

To seed a lawn with grass, the package says to plant 1.75 ounces of grass seed for every square yard of lawn area. About how much grass seed should Vincent buy to seed a square backyard with a side length of 7 yards?

Step 1: Understand the problem.

Read the problem. What does the problem ask you to find?
An estimate for the amount of grass seed Vincent should buy.

What information do you need to solve the problem?
The size of the yard that Vincent wants to seed and the amount of seed that is needed for each square yard.

Step 2: Make a plan.

You know the amount of seed needed for one yard. You want to know the amount for the entire backyard. First, find the area of the backyard using a formula. Then multiply by the amount of seed needed.

This problem does not ask for an exact amount of seed. Multiply using estimation.

Step 3: Follow the plan.

The backyard is a square. The formula for the area of a square is Area = side × side, or $side^2$.

Area = 7 × 7 = 49 square yards

Vincent's backyard has an area of 49 square yards.

Write a multiplication equation. Use words first.

<u>area in square yards</u> <u>times</u> <u>seed weight per yard</u> <u>equals</u> <u>total seed weight</u>

Replace the words with numbers and symbols.

49 sq yd × 1.75 oz per sq yd = total oz

The problem asks for an estimate. Round 49 to the nearest ten, 50. Round 1.75 to the nearest whole number, 2. Then multiply.

50 sq yd × 2 oz per sq yd = 100 oz

Vincent should use about 100 ounces of grass seed.

Step 4: Review.

Does the answer match the question?
Yes. The problem asked for an estimated amount of seed.

There are two types of measurments given in this problem, weight and length.
Is the answer a measurement?
If so, what type?
Yes. The answer is a weight measurement for the amount of grass seed.

? Snow Trails can only manufacture snow when the high temperature for the day is below 28°F. The high temperatures for a week are shown in the following graph. How many of the days shown could Snow Trails have manufactured snow?

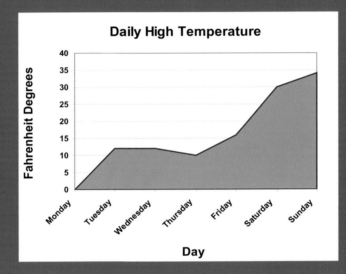

Step 1: Understand the problem.

Read the problem. What does the problem ask you to find?
The number of days on the graph that Snow Trails could have made snow.

What information do you need to solve the problem?
The high temperature for each day and the temperatures at which Snow Trails can make snow.

Is all of the information you need in the problem?
Yes. The problem does not tell you the temperature for each day, but it does give you that information in a graph.

Step 2: Make a plan.

Look at the graph and count the number of days that had a temperature at which snow could be made.

Step 3: Follow the plan.

The problem tells you the high temperature of the day must be less than 28°F. The graph tells you the high temperature in Fahrenheit degrees for each day.

If reading the graph is difficult, try placing something with a straight edge across the graph at about 28°F. Any day that the temperature stays below the straight edge has a high temperature below 28°F. Which days had a temperature below 28°F? **Monday, Tuesday, Wednesday, Thursday, and Friday.**

Count the days listed. There are five.

Snow Trails could have manufactured snow on five of the days shown.

Step 4: Review.

Does the answer match the question?
Yes. The problem asked for a number of days.

㉒ Use a Table

Tina will only go in the pool if the temperature is 25 degrees Celsius or warmer. The thermometer in the pool reads 70 degrees Fahrenheit. Will Tina go in the pool?

Step 1: Understand the problem.

Read the problem. What does the problem ask you to find? **Whether or not Tina will go in the pool.**

Is all of the information that you need in the question? **No. The lowest (coolest) temperature for Tina to go in the pool is given in Celsius degrees. The temperature of the pool is given in Fahrenheit degrees. There is no formula given, or a way to convert the temperatures.**

Step 2: Make a plan.

Find a way to convert the temperature. Let's use a chart or table. Many thermometers are marked in both Celsius and Fahrenheit degrees.

Step 3: Follow the plan.

A section of a table that can be found on your computer or in many books is on the right.

Find 25°C in the Celsius column. What is the equivalent unit in Fahrenheit degrees? **77°F**

Celsius	Fahrenheit
–5	23
0	32
5	41
10	50
15	59
20	68
25	77
30	86

The problem tells you that Tina will not go in the pool unless the water is 25°C, or 77°F or warmer.

Is the pool 77°F or warmer? **No. 70°F is not warmer than 77°F.**

Tina will not go in the pool.

Step 4: Review.

Does the answer match the question?
Yes. The problem asked if Tina would go in the pool.

Is there another way you can solve this problem?
Yes. You could have converted the pool temperature to Celsius and compared the temperatures in Celsius degrees.
Let's use a formula to try. The formula is °C = (5/9)(°F − 32).
Substitute in 70°F.   °C = (5/9)(70 − 32)
                           °C = (5/9)(38)
                           °C = 21 $\frac{1}{9}$

The Celsius temperature of the pool is less than 25° degrees

㉓ Time Basics

Time is measured just as other measurements are. The measuring tools of time are clocks and calendars instead of scales or rulers.

Units of Time

Some units of time are always the same, or constant. There are always exactly 60 seconds in one minute. Others can vary. Some months have 30 days, others have 31. Because time is so important, it will help you to memorize the units of time.

Constant Units	Units that Vary
second (sec or s)	1 month (mo) =
1 minute (min) = 60 seconds	28, 29, 30, or 31 days
1 hour (hr or h) = 60 minutes	
1 day (d) = 24 hours	1 year (yr) = 12 months =
1 week (wk) = 7 days	365 or 366 days

Every year has 12 months. In order, the months are: **January (Jan), February (Feb), March (Mar), April (Apr), May, June, July, August (Aug), September (Sept), October (Oct), November (Nov), December (Dec).**

The months of April, June, September, and November each have 30 days. The months with 31 days are January, March, May, July, August, October, and December. February has 28 days most years, but every fourth year, called a leap year, it has 29 days.

A.M. and P.M.

The 24 hours in a day are usually counted in two sets of twelve.

Starting at 12 o'clock midnight and ending just before 12 o'clock noon the hours are followed by the term A.M. (ante meridiem, before midday).

Starting at 12 o'clock noon and ending just before 12 o'clock midnight the hours are followed by the term P.M. (post meridiem, after midday).

Be careful!

A day is the period of time from one midnight to the next midnight.

The word "day" can also be used to mean the part of the day when the a person is at school or at work. Sometimes the word "day" is also used to mean the time when the sun is in the sky.

Clayton can get his driver's license this year on his birthday, June 4th. If today is April 28th, how many more days are there until Clayton's birthday?

Step 1: Understand the problem.

Read the problem. Is there anything you do not understand?

What does the problem ask you to find?
The number of days from April 28th until June 4th.

Is all of the information you need in the problem?
No. You know the dates. To solve the problem, you need to know the number of days in April and May. There are 30 days in April and 31 days in May.

Step 2: Make a plan.

Break the problem into parts. Add up the number of days in April, May, and June that are between April 28th and June 4th.

Step 3: Follow the plan.

Begin with today's date, April 28th.
There are 30 days in April. From April 28th until April 30th, there are 2 days.

After April is May. All of May is between April 28th and June 4th.
There are 31 days in May.

After May is June.
From June 1st to June 4th, there are 4 days.

Add the number of days for each month.

April days + May days + June days = total

   2   +   31   +   4   = 37

There are 37 days until Clayton's birthday.

Step 4: Review.

Does the answer match the question?
Yes. The question asks for the number of days until Clayton's birthday.

Is there another way to solve the problem?
Yes. You could look at a calendar and count the number of days.

Twila put a cake in the oven to bake at 10:55 A.M. She took it out at 11:57 A.M. How long did the cake bake?

Step 1: Understand the problem.

Read the problem. Is there anything you do not understand?

What does the problem ask you to find?
The length of time the cake baked.

Do you have all of the information you need to solve the problem?
Yes. You know what time the cake was put in the oven and what time the cake was taken out of the oven.

Step 2: Make a plan.

Problems that ask how much time has passed, or elapsed, between two given times can be solved by counting on from the starting time to the ending time.

Step 3: Follow the plan.

Follow the plan. Begin with the time the cake was put into the oven. Count the whole hours.

10:55, 11:55
        1

10:55 A.M. to 11:55 A.M. is 1 hour.

Count the minutes from 11:55 to 11:57.

11:55, 11:56, 11:57
        1   2

11:55 A.M. to 11:57 A.M. is 2 minutes.

Combine the hours and minutes.

1 hour 2 minutes

The cake baked for 1 hour 2 minutes.

Step 4: Review.

Does the answer match the question?
Yes. The problem asked for the amount of time the cake baked.

Is the answer reasonable? **Yes. Depending on the type of cake being baked, a little over an hour is a reasonable amount of time.**

㉖ Time Zones

It is 9:00 P.M. in Denver, Colorado, where Evan lives. Evan's aunt lives in Boston, Massachusetts. Is it a good time for Evan to call his aunt?

Step 1: Understand the problem.

Read the problem. What does the problem ask you to find?
If it is a good time for Evan to call his aunt.

Do you have all of the information you need to solve the problem?
No. You need to know what time it is in Boston.

Step 2: Make a plan.

You can use a time zone map to find the number of time zones between Denver and Boston.

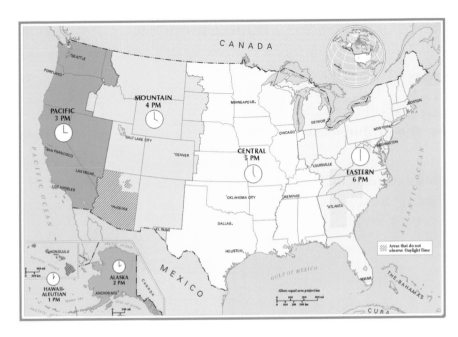

Step 3: Follow the plan.

The world is divided into 24 time zones. Time zones that are west of you are earlier by one hour per time zone. Time zones that are east of you are later by one hour per time zone. Denver is in the Mountain Standard Time Zone. Boston is two time zones east of Denver, in the Eastern Standard Time Zone. It is two hours later in Boston than it is in Denver.

9:00 P.M. + 2 hours is 11:00 P.M.

Since it is 11:00 P.M. in Boston, it might be too late for Evan to call his aunt.

Step 4: Review.

Does your answer make sense? **Yes. The sun rises in the east, so areas to the east are going to always be farther along in amount of daylight than those to the west. This means that daylight also ends in the east before it does in the west. The daylight period of a day ends about 2 hours earlier in Boston than it does in Denver.**

57

Morgan took 9 minutes 32 seconds to type a 300-word essay. Don took 8 minutes 51 seconds to type the same essay. How much longer did Morgan take to type the essay than Don?

Step 1: Understand the problem.

Read the problem. Is there anything you do not understand?

What does the problem ask you to find?
The difference in the amount of time it took Morgan and Don to type the essay.

Do you have all of the information you need to solve the problem?
Yes. You know how long each person took.

Step 2: Make a plan.

Problems that ask questions like *how much longer* and *how much more* are usually subtraction problems. Write a subtraction equation.

Step 3: Follow the plan.

Write the problem in words.

Morgan's time minus Don's time equals difference in time

Replace the words with numbers and symbols.

9 minutes 32 seconds − 8 minutes 51 seconds = difference in time

This problem uses both minutes and seconds. Only add or subtract measurement units that are the same. Subtract seconds from seconds and minutes from minutes. You can regroup units as you do when you subtract whole numbers. Remember, there are 60 seconds in one minute.

```
     8          92
     9̶ minutes 3̶2̶ seconds    Subtract seconds first. Convert one
   − 8 minutes 51 seconds    minute into seconds.
               41 seconds
```

Morgan took 41 seconds longer than Don to type the essay.

Step 4: Review.

Does your answer make sense? **Yes. Morgan took a little more than 9 1/2 minutes. Don took a little less than 9 minutes. The difference should be a little more than half a minute.**

Check your answer by counting up from Don's time to Morgan's time or by using addition. **If you count up from Don's time, the count could go like this:**

Start: 8 min 51 sec
       9 min 1 sec   10 sec
       9 min 11 sec   20 sec
       9 min 21 sec   30 sec
       9 min 31 sec   40 sec
       9 min 32 sec   41 sec

Jerome will camp in four states over his vacation. He will spend 1 week 3 days in each state. How much time will he camp in those four states in all?

Step 1: Understand the problem.

Read the problem. Is there anything you do not understand?

What does the problem ask you to find?
The total amount of time Jerome will camp in the four states.

Do you have all of the information you need to solve the problem?
Yes. You know know how long Jerome is camping in each state.

Step 2: Make a plan.

Jerome is camping the same amount of time in each state. This is a multiplication problem. Let's write a multiplication equation.

Step 3: Follow the plan.

Write the problem in words.

time in each state times number of states equals total time

Replace the words with numbers and symbols.

1 week 3 days × 4 = total time

This problem uses both weeks and days. You can multiply in two ways.

One way: Multiply and regroup units as you do with whole numbers.

Another way: Convert to all one unit, then multiply.

Multiply the mixed units, and regroup as you multiply.

$$
\begin{array}{r}
1 \\
1 \text{ week } \quad 3 \text{ days} \\
\times \quad\quad\quad 4 \\
\hline
5 \text{ days}
\end{array}
$$

3 days × 4 = 12 days = 1 week 5 days
Carry over the week that was regrouped.

$$
\begin{array}{r}
1 \\
1 \text{ week } \quad 3 \text{ days} \\
\times \quad\quad\quad 4 \\
\hline
5 \text{ weeks } \quad 5 \text{ days}
\end{array}
$$

1 week × 4 = 4 weeks
Add the week that was regrouped.

Jerome will be camping in the four states for 5 weeks 5 days in all.

Step 4: Review.

Does the answer match the question?
Yes. The problem asked for a time in all.

Try changing to all days, then multiplying.
1 week 3 days = 10 days
10 days × 4 = 40 days
40 days = 5 weeks 5 days

61

Further Reading

Books

Fandel, Jennifer. *The Metric System.* Mankato, Minn.: Creative Education, 2006.

O'Donnell, Kerri. *Natural Wonders of the World: Converting Measurements to Metric Units.* New York: Rosen Pub., 2005.

Sullivan, Navin. *Area, Distance, and Volume.* New York: Marshall Cavendish Benchmark, 2007.

More math help from Rebecca Wingard-Nelson:

Wingard-Nelson, Rebecca. *Problem Solving and Word Problems.* Berkeley Heights, N.J.: Enslow Publishers, Inc., 2004.

Internet Addresses

Banfill, J. *AAA Math.* "Measurement." © 2009. <http://www.aaamath.com/mea.html>

Gamequarium. "Measurement Games." © 2000–2007. <http://www.gamequarium.com/measurement.html>

Math.com. "Unit Conversion." © 2000–2005. <http://www.math.com/tables/general/measures.htm>

Index

A
adding measurements, 25
area, 26–27

C
calendars, 52–53
capacity, 10–11, 28–29, 30–31,
    32–33, 34
changing dimensions, 36–37
converting units
    days to weeks, 61
    feet to miles, 16–17
    feet to yards, 14–15
    kilometers to meters, 18–19
    liters to deciliters, 31
    meters to centimeters, 23
    meters to kilometers, 19
    minutes to seconds, 59
    pints to gallons, 28–29
    temperature, 48–49
    weeks to days, 61
cubes, 36–37

D
direct measurement, 23
dividing measurements, 31, 37
draw a picture, 24, 35

E
elapsed time, 54–55
error, 32–33
    greatest possible, 32

estimation
    length, 20–21
    weight, 44–45

F
formulas, 34–35, 44, 49
fractions, 16–17

G
graphs, 46–47
gravity, 39

I
indirect measurement, 23

L
length, 10–11, 12–13, 14–15,
    16–17, 18–19, 20–21,
    22–23

M
mass, 10–11, 38–39, 42–43
mental math, 42–43
metric units, 11, 18–19, 30–31,
    32–33, 34–35, 42–43
multiplying measurements, 27,
    29, 35, 36, 39, 40–41,
    44–45, 60–61

P
perimeter, 24–25
precision, 32

problem-solving steps, 8–9
problem-solving tips, 6–7

S
standard units, 10, 12–13,
    14–15, 16–17, 28–29, 38–39,
    40–41
subtracting measurements,
    22–23, 59

T
tables, 48–49
temperature, 46–47, 48–49
time
    A.M. and P.M., 51
    calendars, 52–53
    elapsed, 54–55
    units, 50–51
time zones, 56–57

V
volume, 34–35, 36–37

W
weight, 10, 38–39, 40–41
write an equation, 15, 23, 24–25,
    29, 31, 38–39, 40, 44–45, 59,
    60–61